WITHDRAWN

JAN 2 0 2010

W9-AHO-574

VOCAL SELECTIONS

CHILDREN OF EDEN

Music and Lyrics by
STEPHEN SCHWARTZ

The offering of this publication for sale is not to be construed as authorization for the performance of any material contained herein. Applications for the right to perform Children of Eden, in whole or in part, should be addressed to:

MUSIC THEATRE INTERNATIONAL
421 W. 54th St., New York, New York 10019. Tel. 212/541-4MTI • Fax 212/FX7-4MTI
Website www.MTISHOWS.com

ISBN-13: 978-1-4234-1104-8
ISBN-10: 1-4234-1104-8

WILLIAMSON MUSIC®
A RODGERS AND HAMMERSTEIN COMPANY
www.williamsonmusic.com

EXCLUSIVELY DISTRIBUTED BY

HAL•LEONARD®
CORPORATION

7777 W. BLUEMOUND RD. P.O. BOX 13819 MILWAUKEE, WI 53213

In Australia Contact:
Hal Leonard Australia Pty. Ltd.
4 Lentara Court
Cheltenham, Victoria, 3192 Australia
Email: ausadmin@halleonard.com

Williamson Music is a registered trademark of the Family Trust u/w Richard Rodgers and the Estate of Oscar Hammerstein II.

For all works contained herein:
Unauthorized copying, arranging, adapting, recording or public performance is an infringement of copyright.
Infringers are liable under the law.

Visit Hal Leonard Online at
www.halleonard.com

CONTENTS

STEPHEN SCHWARTZ

Stephen Schwartz has contributed music and/or lyrics to *Wicked*, *Godspell*, *Pippin*, *The Magic Show*, *The Baker's Wife*, *Working* (which he also adapted and directed), *Personals*, *Rags*, and *Children of Eden*. He collaborated with Leonard Bernstein on the English texts for Bernstein's *Mass* and wrote the title song for the play and movie *Butterflies Are Free*. For films, he wrote the songs for the DreamWorks animated feature *Prince of Egypt* and collaborated with Alan Menken on the scores for the Disney animated features *Pocahontas* and *The Hunchback of Notre Dame*. For children, he has written a one-act musical, *Captain Louie*, and a picture book, *The Perfect Peach*. Mr. Schwartz has released two CDs of original songs entitled *Reluctant Pilgrim* and *Uncharted Territory*. Among the awards he has received are three Academy Awards, four Grammy Awards, four Drama Desk Awards, and a Golden Globe.

THE SPARK OF CREATION

Music and Lyrics by
STEPHEN SCHWARTZ

Steady, driving tempo ♩ = 176

1. I've got an itch-ing on the tips of my fin - gers.
2. I see a moun-tain and I want to climb__ it.

I've got a boil-ing in the back of my brain.__ I've got a hun - ger
I see a riv - er and I want to leave shore.__ Where there was noth - ing,

Copyright © 1991 Grey Dog Music (administered by Williamson Music)
International Copyright Secured   All Rights Reserved

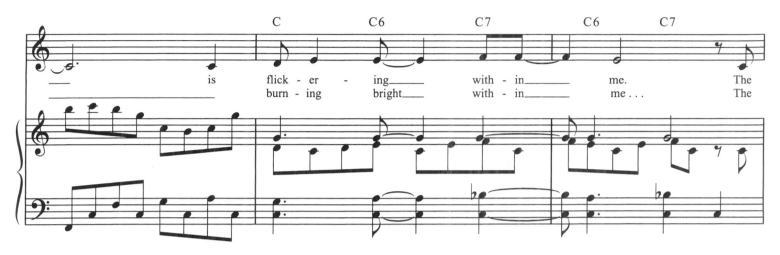

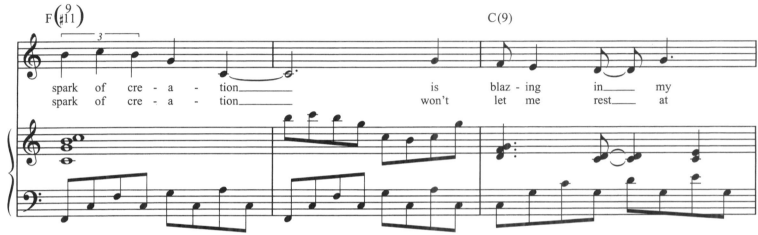

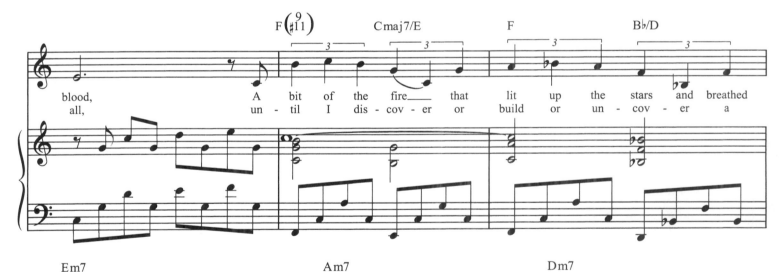

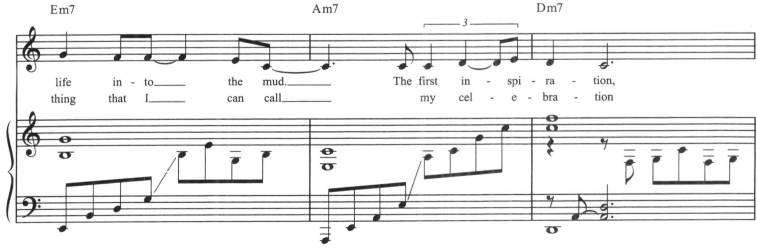

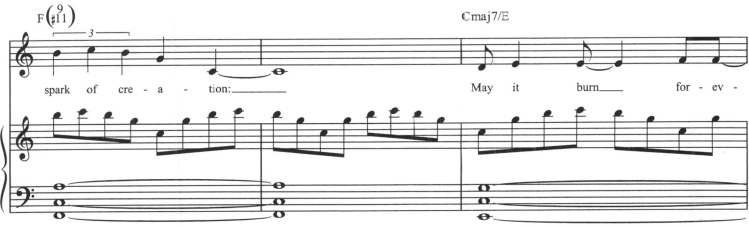

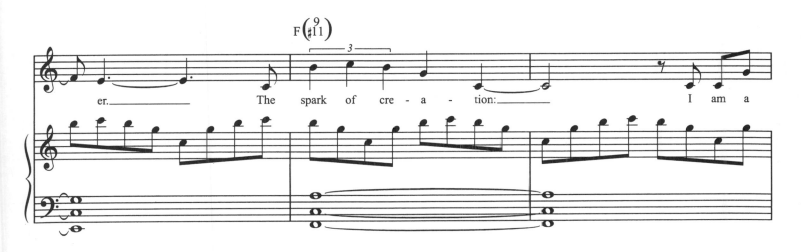

keep - er of___ the flame. We think all we want is a

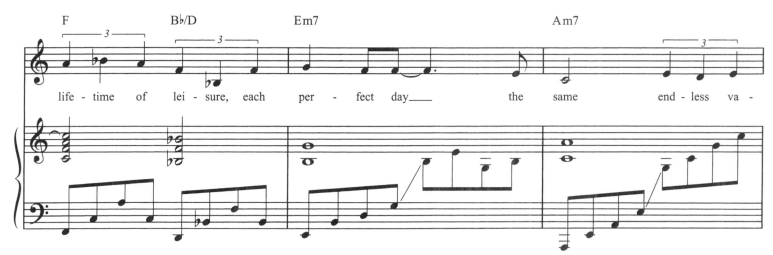

life - time of lei - sure, each per - fect day___ the same end - less va -

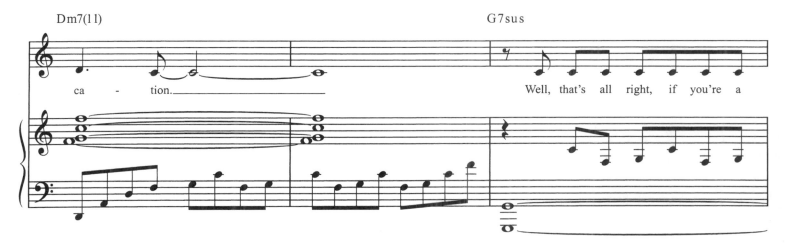

ca - tion._____ Well, that's all right, if you're a

kind of crus - ta - cean, but when you're born with an i - mag - i - na - tion,

soon - er or la - ter, you're feel - ing the fire_____ get hot - ter and high - er...

The spark of_____

C   C6   C7   C6   C7

C   C6   C7   C6   C7   F(9/#11)   Cmaj7/E

cre - a - tion!_____

C#   B   G(4)   C

IN PURSUIT OF EXCELLENCE

Music and Lyrics by
STEPHEN SCHWARTZ

Misterioso (♩ = 92)

Copyright © 1991 Grey Dog Music (administered by Williamson Music)
International Copyright Secured   All Rights Reserved

Astaire style, easy swing (♩ = 98)

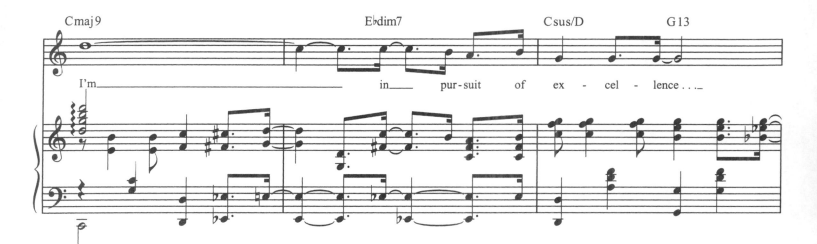

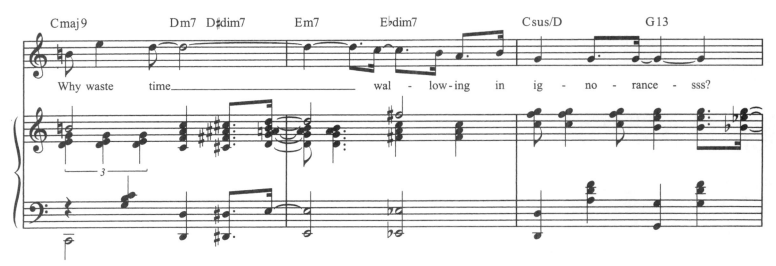

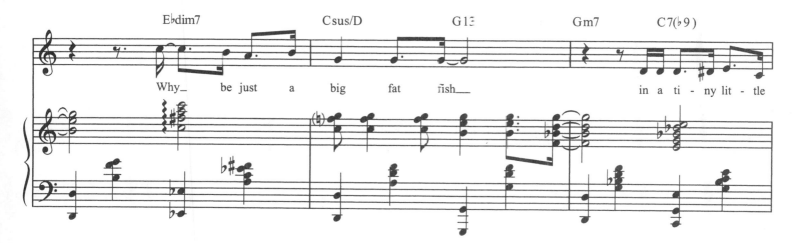

Why_ be just a big fat fish_ in a ti - ny lit - tle

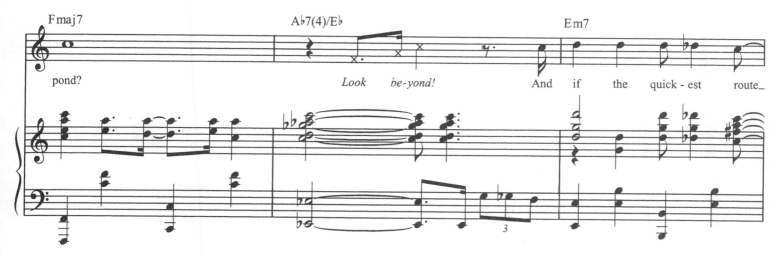

pond? *Look be-yond!* And if the quick - est route_

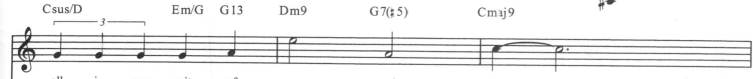

means a taste of for - bid - den fruit,_____ what the hey! It's

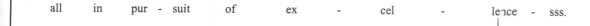

all in pur - suit of ex - cel - lence - sss.

(SNAKE)

So . . . Don't be such a stiff.___

Mmm, just take a sniff.___ Real - ly, what's the diff',___

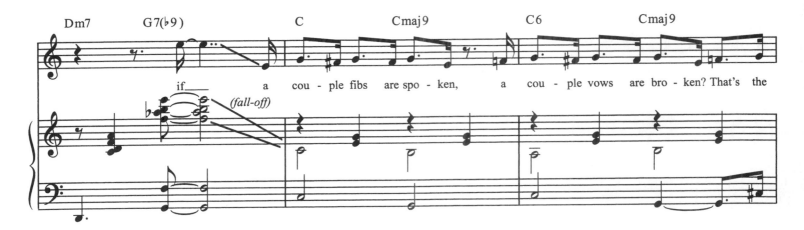

if___ a cou - ple fibs are spo - ken, a cou - ple vows are bro - ken? That's the

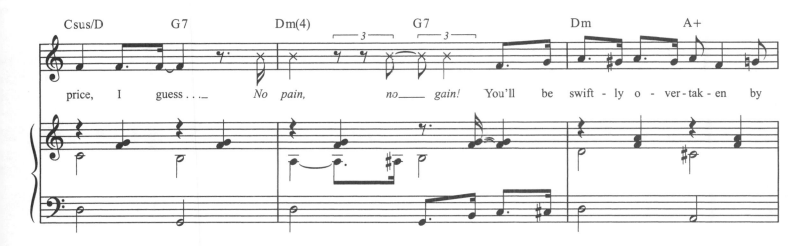

price, I guess.... *No pain,* *no gain!* You'll be swift-ly o-ver-tak-en by

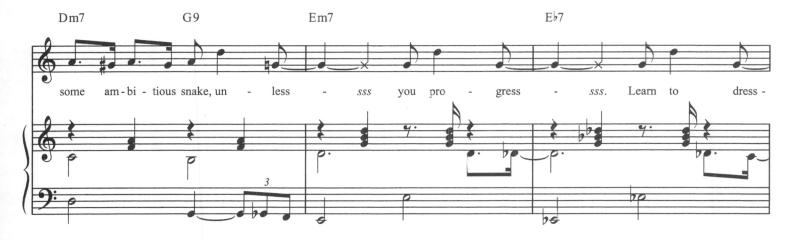

some am-bi-tious snake, un-less -sss you pro-gress -sss. Learn to dress-

sss for suc-cess-sss. Yes -sss!

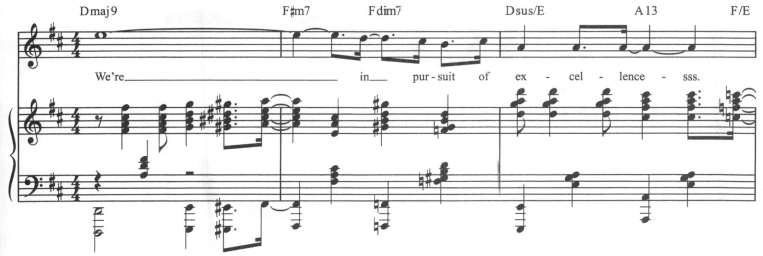

We're_____ in__ pur-suit of ex-cel-lence -sss.

Winners dare to take the risk - sss, while the los - ers dis -

(SNAKE)

cuss - sss . . . *That's why they're los - ers!* Pass the test___ when you're test - ed.

Be the best,___ not the best - ed.

Let oth - er ner - vous wrecks - sss stay too fright - end to stick out their

necks - sss. They're not in pur - suit of ex - cel - lence - sss like

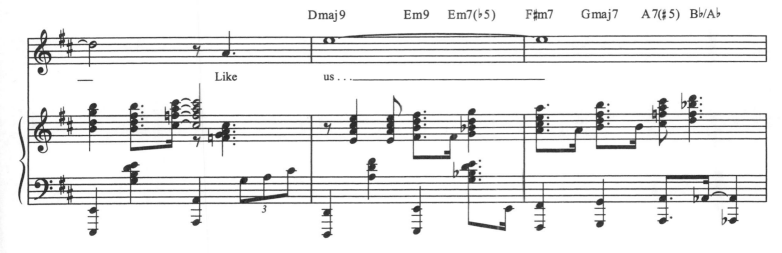

us . . . . Like us . . .

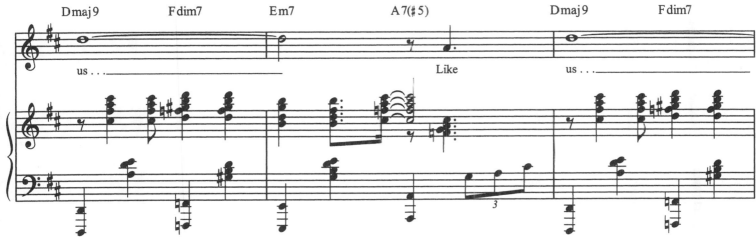

Like us . . . .

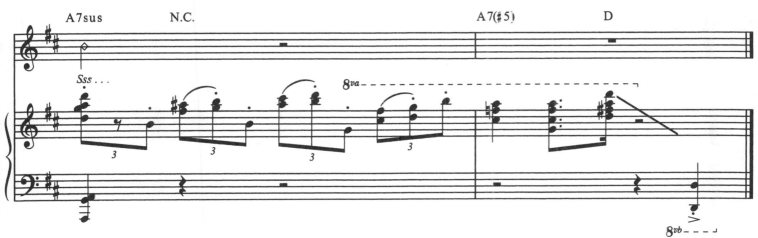

Sss . . .

A WORLD WITHOUT YOU

Music and Lyrics by
STEPHEN SCHWARTZ

Moderately slow (♩ = 76)

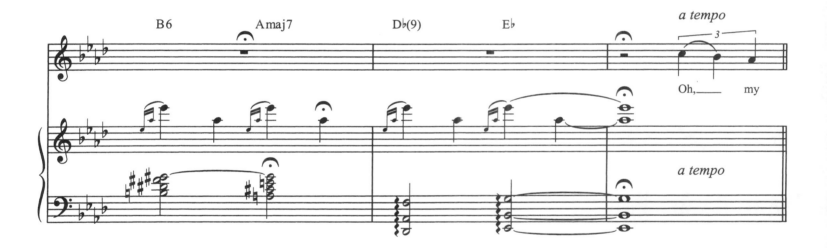

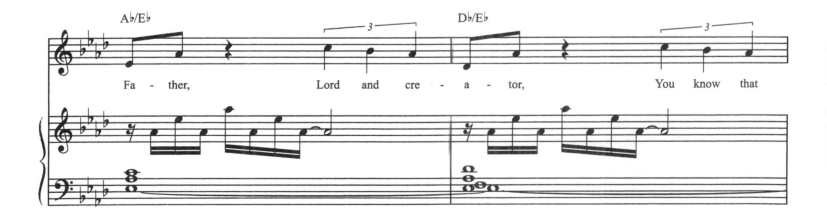

Copyright © 1991 Grey Dog Music (administered by Williamson Music)
International Copyright Secured   All Rights Reserved

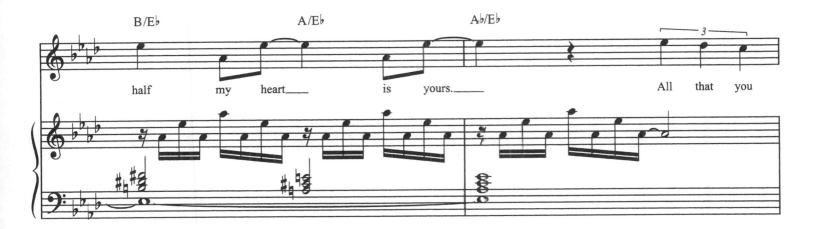

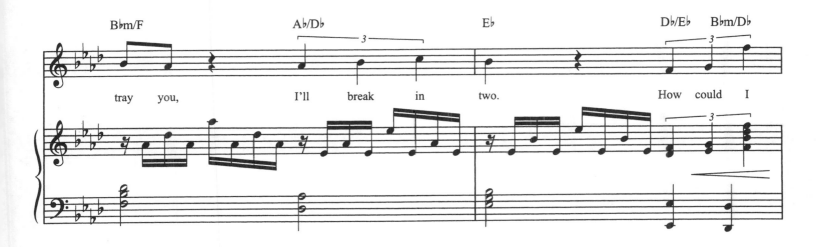

But oh, my life's part - ner, my wife, my

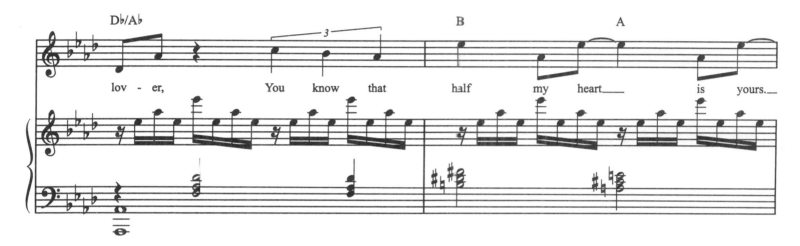

lov - er, You know that half my heart___ is yours.___

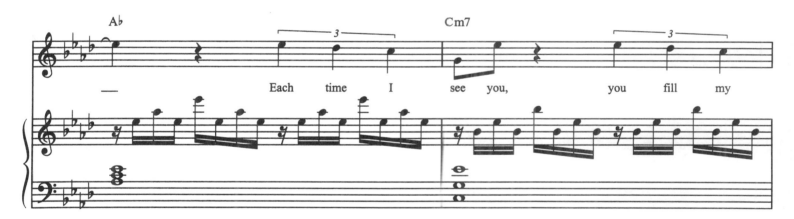

___ Each time I see you, you fill my

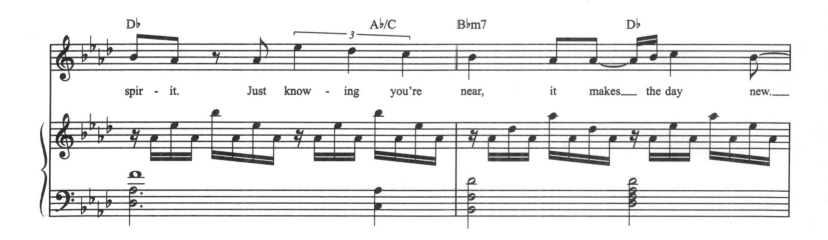

spir - it. Just know - ing you're near, it makes___ the day new.___

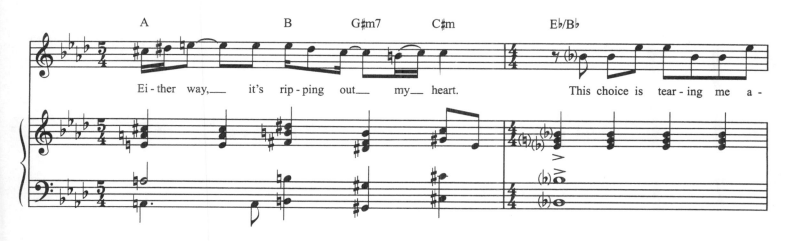

THE WASTELAND

Music and Lyrics by
STEPHEN SCHWARTZ

Moderately ♩ = 100

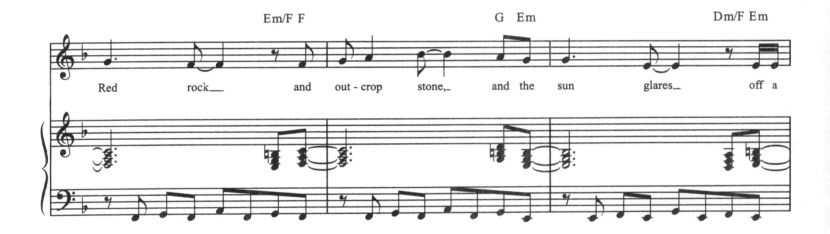

Red rock___ and out-crop stone,___ and the sun glares___ off a

bleach-ing bone.___ There's no com-fort or soft-ness here; there's on-ly the

Copyright © 1991 Grey Dog Music (administered by Williamson Music)
International Copyright Secured   All Rights Reserved

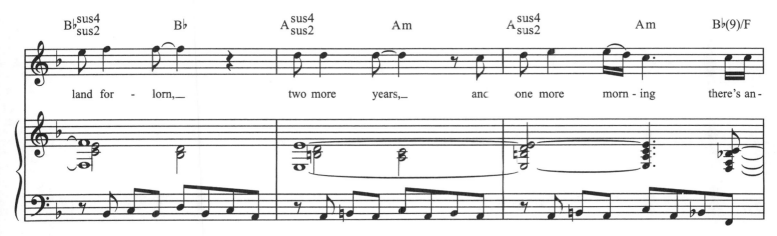

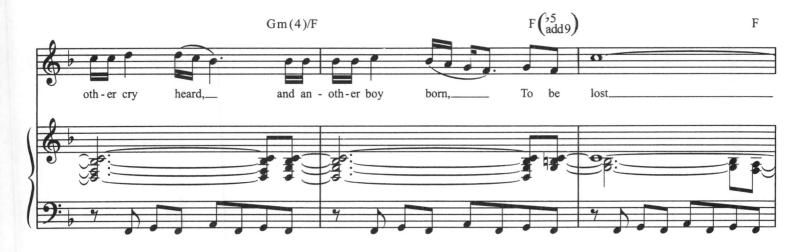

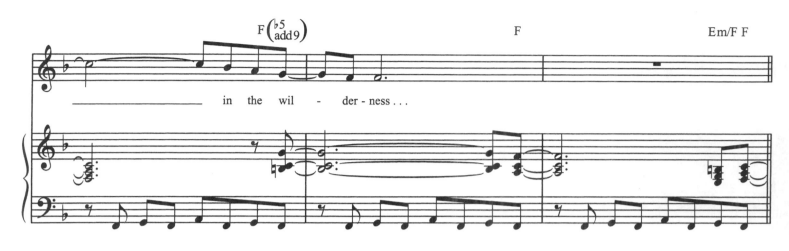

in the wil - der - ness . . .

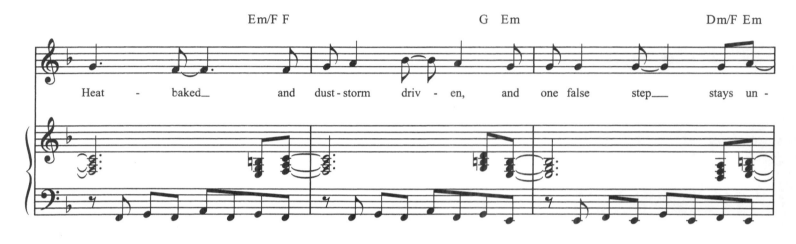

Heat - baked___ and dust-storm driv - en, and one false step___ stays un -

for - giv - en. And all that you know___ is you weren't made to live___ in the

Repeat and fade

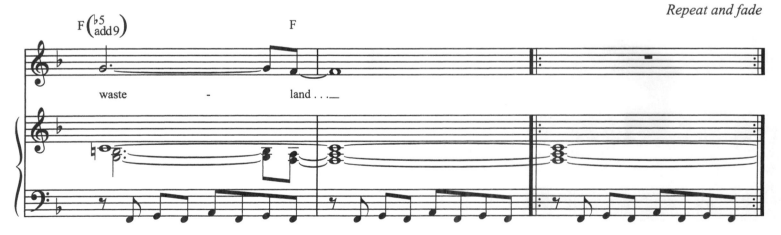

waste - land . . .___

LOST IN THE WILDERNESS

Music and Lyrics by
STEPHEN SCHWARTZ

Rock ♩ = 120

Verse:

1. I never made this world. I didn't even lose it.
2. You follow all the rules, you swallow all the stories

Copyright © 1991 Grey Dog Music (administered by Williamson Music)
International Copyright Secured   All Rights Reserved

CLOSE TO HOME

Music and Lyrics by
STEPHEN SCHWARTZ

Copyright © 1991 Grey Dog Music (administered by Williamson Music)
International Copyright Secured   All Rights Reserved

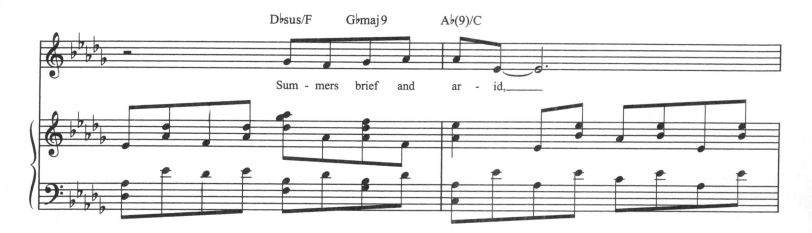

Sum-mers brief and ar-id,_____

win-ters bleak and numb,

look what we call

home.

These old walls are stained and scarred._

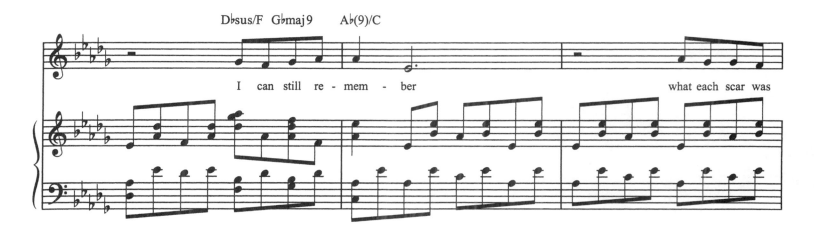

I can still re-mem-ber

what each scar was

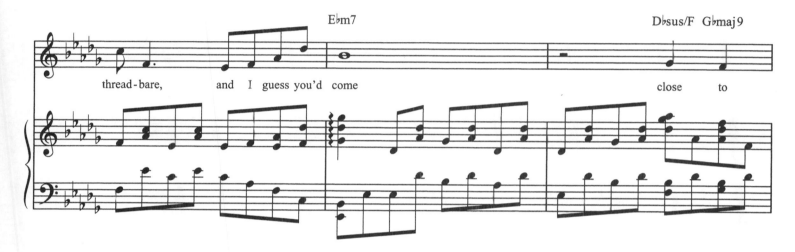

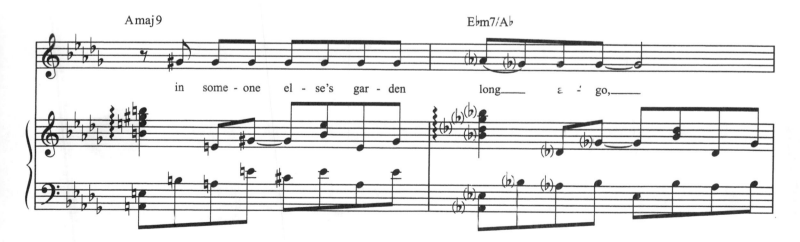

we had all___ we could eat.___ But it seems the fruit our

own hands grow___ some - how tastes__ twice as sweet._____

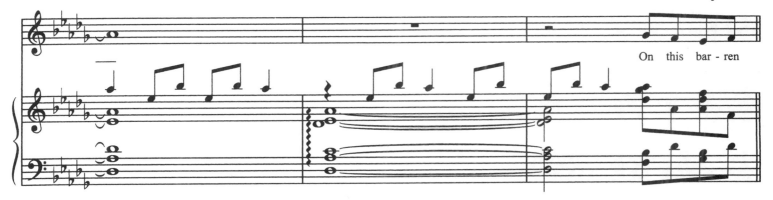

On this bar - ren

plot we'll plant our wheat and dig our wells,_

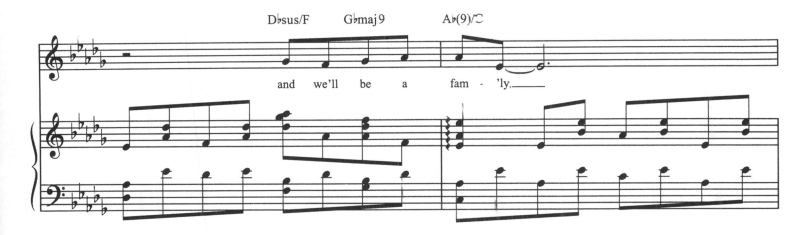

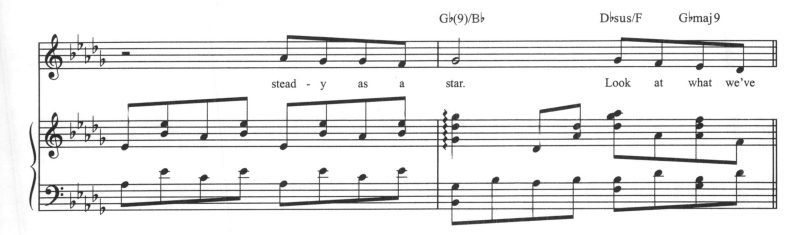

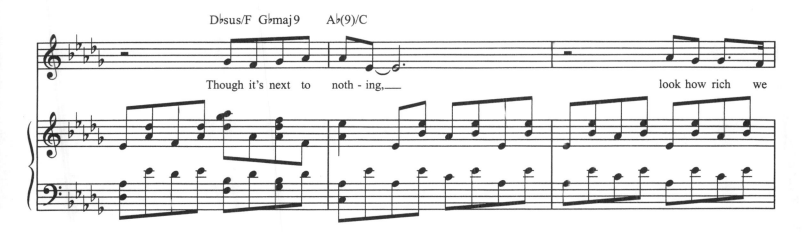

Broader

are. Fun - ny now how E - den does-n't seem so far ...

Come sit be - side me in the dy - ing light.___

What storms the morn - ing brings, we'll weath - er all___ right.___

Your hand in my___ hand, and as we sit here

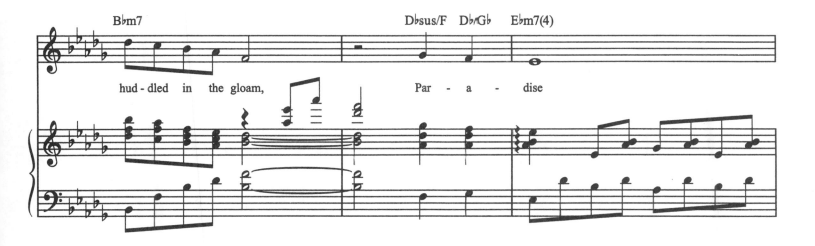

hud - dled in the gloam,   Par - a - dise

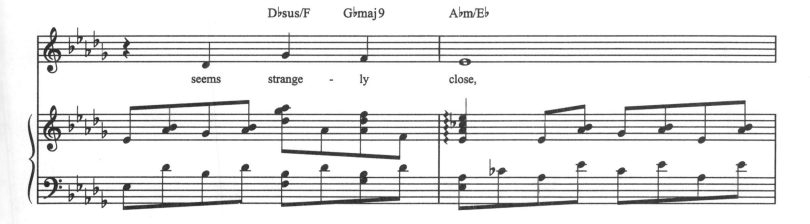

seems   strange - ly   close,

close   to   home,   close   to

home.   3,   2,   1,   now   we   all   go   home.

rall.

CHILDREN OF EDEN

Music and Lyrics by
STEPHEN SCHWARTZ

Rubato

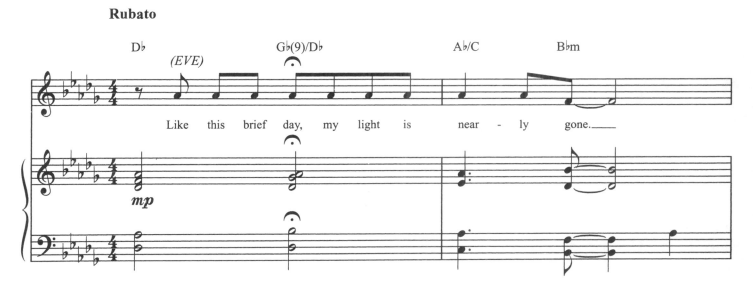

Like this brief day, my light is near-ly gone.___

But through the night,___ my chil-dren, you will go on.___

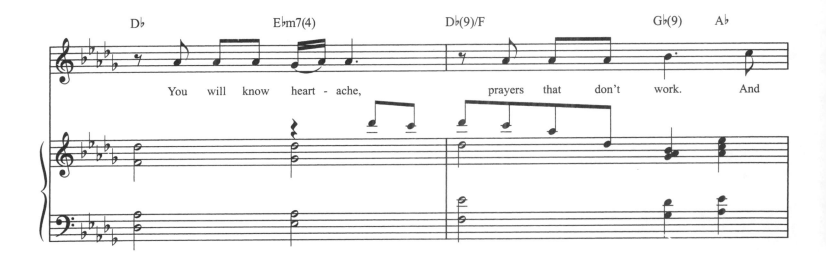

You will know heart-ache, prayers that don't work. And

Copyright © 1991 Grey Dog Music (administered by Williamson Music)
International Copyright Secured   All Rights Reserved

44

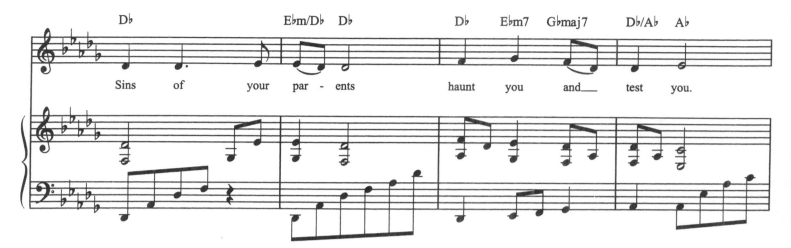

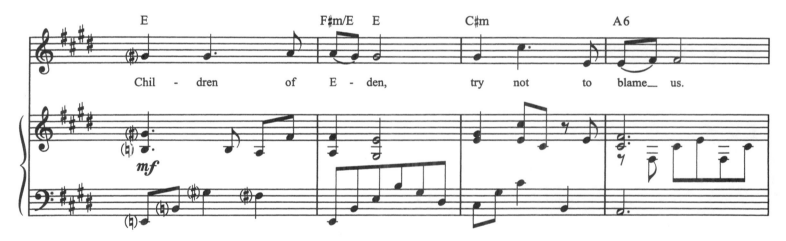

STRANGER TO THE RAIN

Music and Lyrics by
STEPHEN SCHWARTZ

With controlled emotion (♩ = 104) (♪ = ♪)

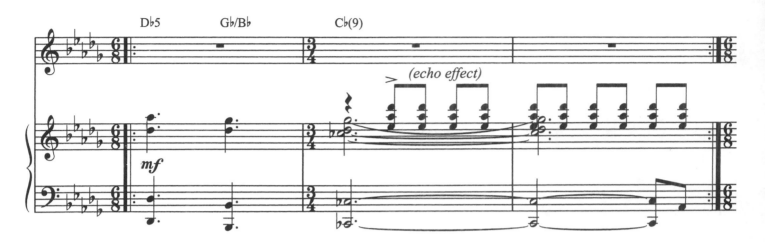

(YONAH)

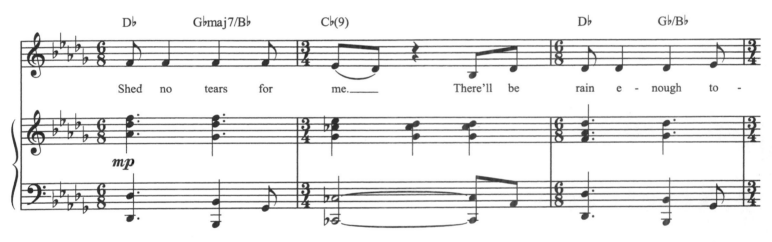

Shed no tears for me.___ There'll be rain e - nough to -

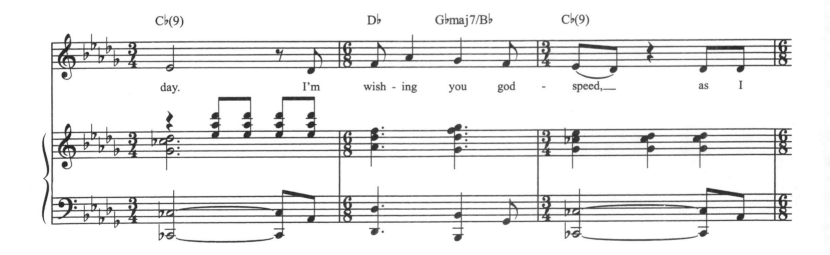

day. I'm wish - ing you god - speed,___ as I

Copyright © 1991 Grey Dog Music (administered by Williamson Music)
International Copyright Secured   All Rights Reserved

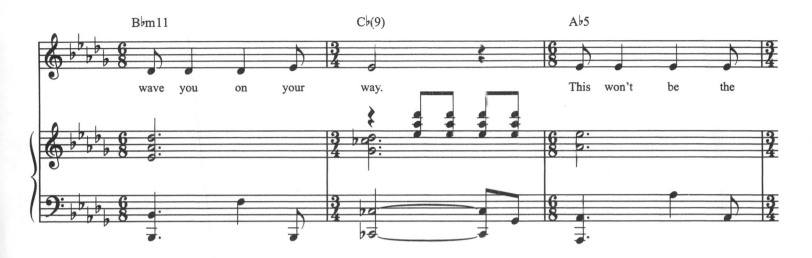

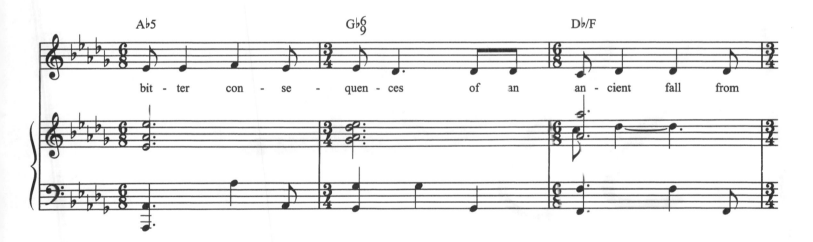

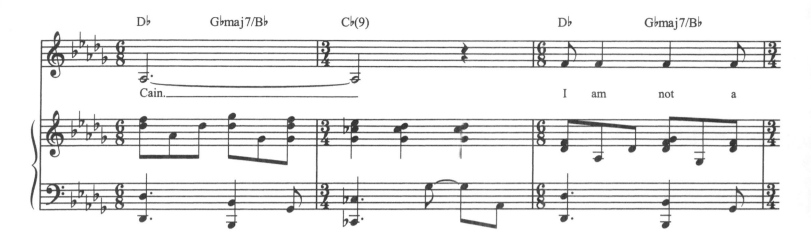

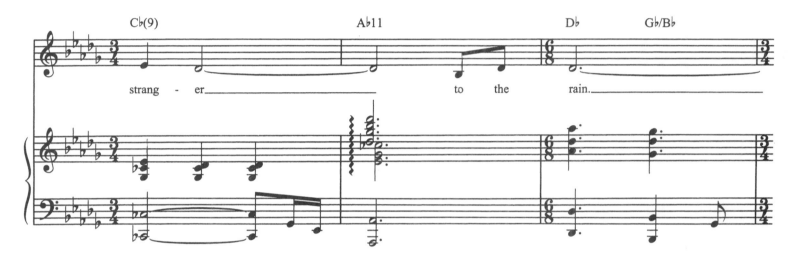

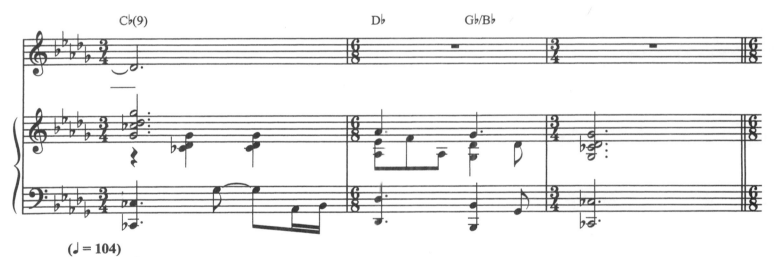

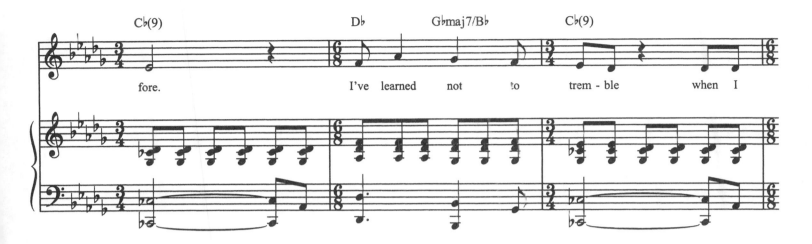

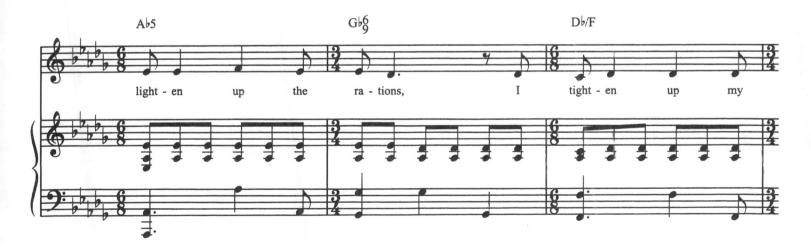

50

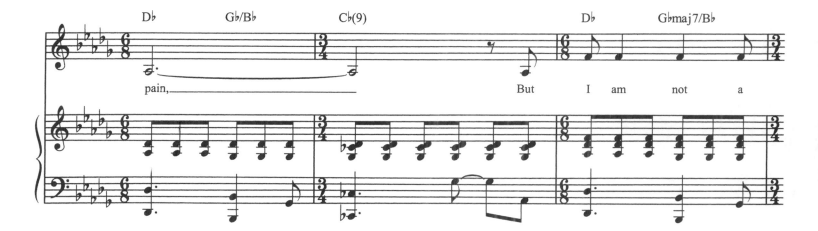

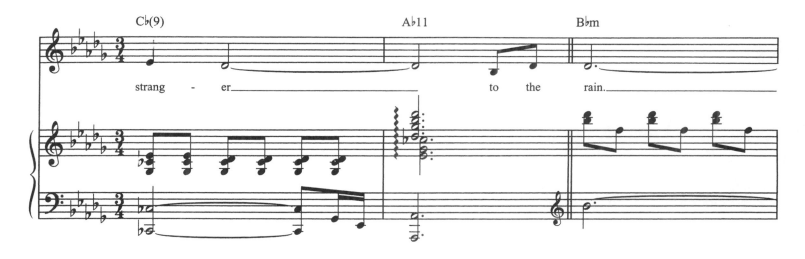

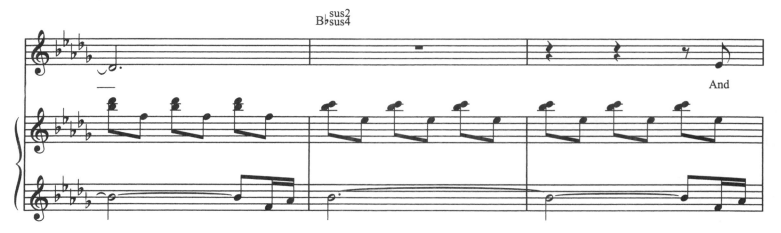

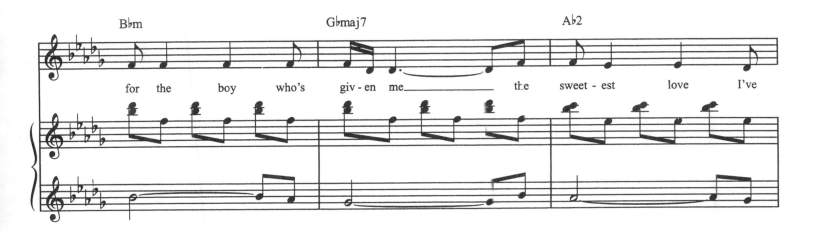

for the boy who's giv-en me_____ the sweet-est love I've

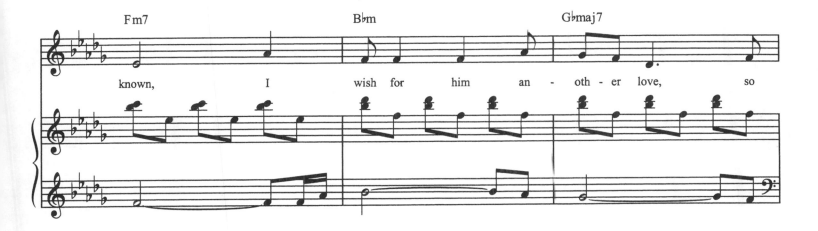

known, I wish for him an-oth-er love, so

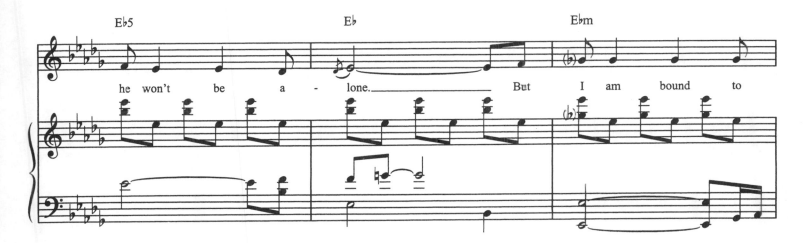

he won't be a-lone._____ But I am bound to

walk a-mong the wound-ed and the slain. And

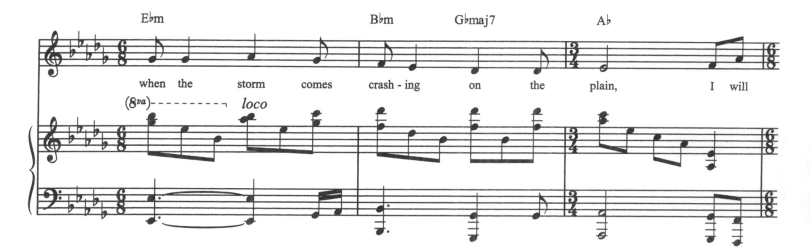

when the storm comes crash-ing on the plain, I will

dance be-fore the light-ning, to mu-sic sa-cred and pro-

fane. Oh,

shed no tears for me. Light no

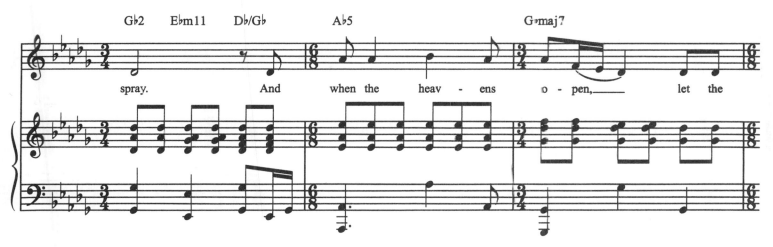

drops fall where they__ may. If they fi - n'lly wash a -

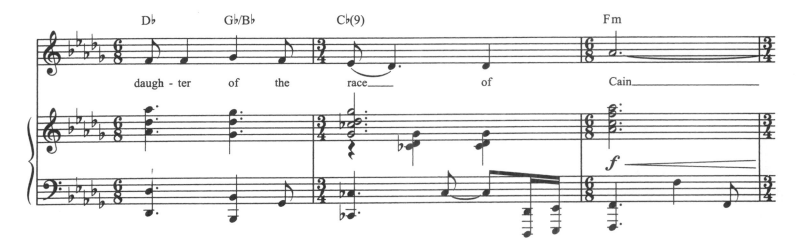

way the stain_____ from a

daugh - ter of the race_____ of Cain_____

___ I_____ am not a

55

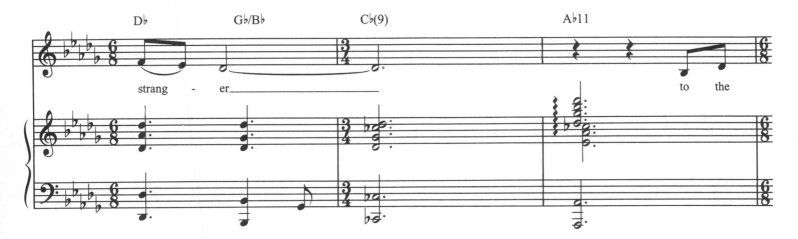

strang - er_____ to the

rain._____

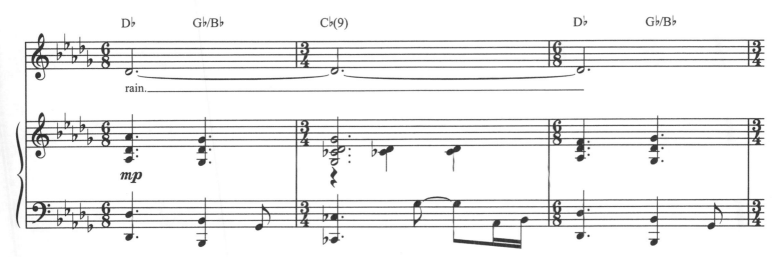

Let___ it rain . . ._____

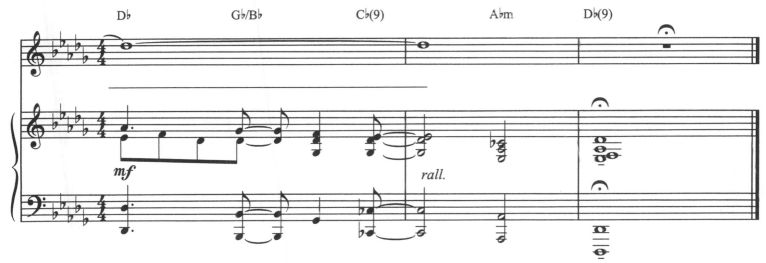

mf   rall.

IN WHATEVER TIME WE HAVE

Music and Lyrics by
STEPHEN SCHWARTZ

Flowing, with sincerity and simplicity ♩ = 112

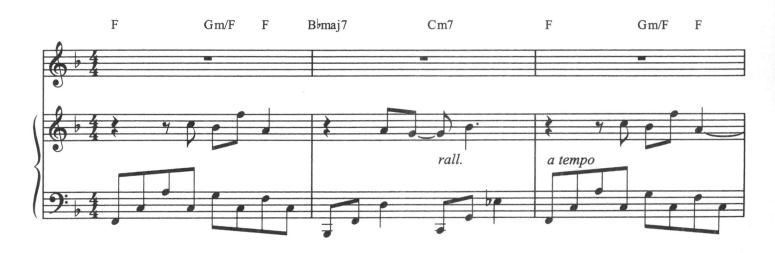

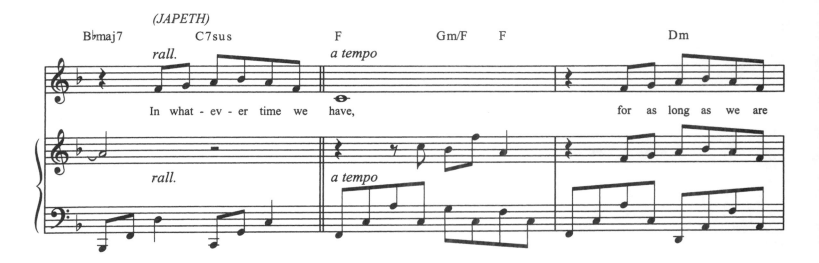

(JAPETH)

In what-ev-er time we have, for as long as we are

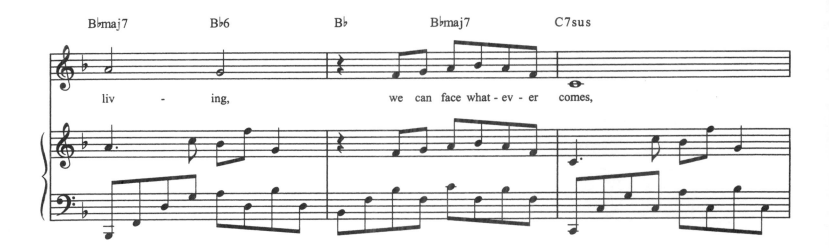

liv - ing, we can face what-ev - er comes,

Copyright © 1991 Grey Dog Music (administered by Williamson Music)
International Copyright Secured   All Rights Reserved

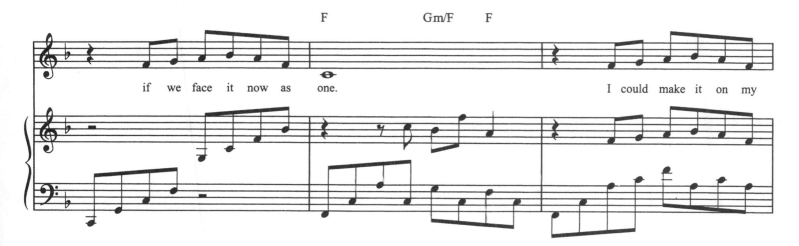

F   Gm/F   F

if we face it now as one.   I could make it on my

Am   B♭

own;   let me know that I don't have   to.

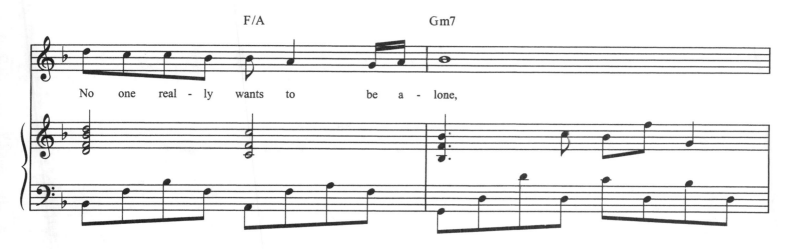

F/A   Gm7

No one real - ly wants to be a - lone,

B♭maj7   C7sus

in what - ev - er time we have.   1. If at times we are a -

(l.v.)

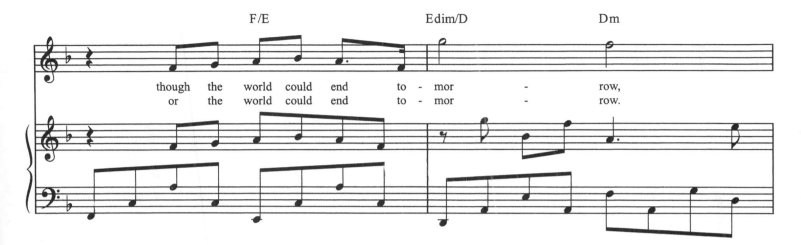

though the world could end to - mor - row,
or the world could end to - mor - row.

you and I will be to - geth - er in what -

ev - er time we have.

We know life can__ be a

bat - tle - field, but we won't run____ and we won't yield.__

____ You'll be____ my for - tress,____ and I____

____ will be your shield. No one real - ly wants to be a - lone,____

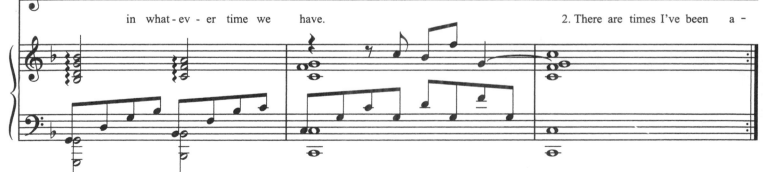

in what - ev - er time we have. 2. There are times I've been a -

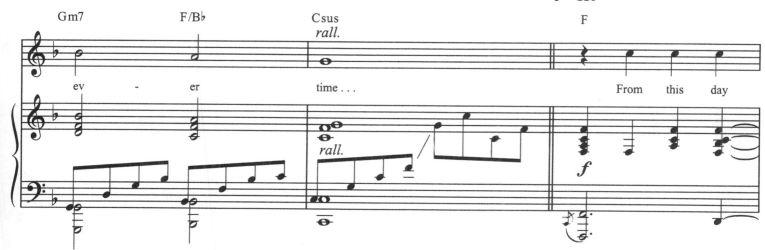

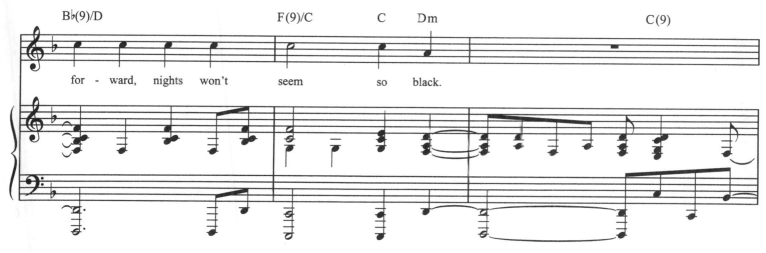

THE HARDEST PART OF LOVE

Music and Lyrics by
STEPHEN SCHWARTZ

Con moto (♩ = 92)

Rubato

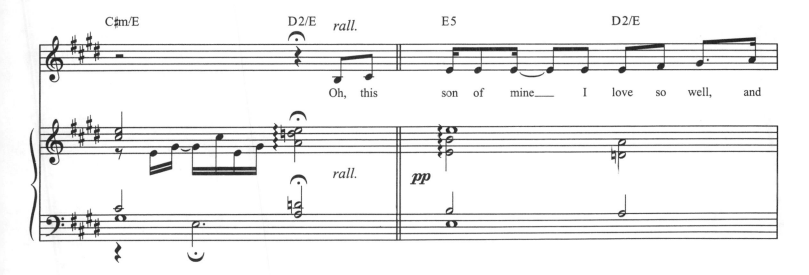

Oh, this son of mine___ I love so well, and
oh, the toll it takes. I would give to him___ a gar - den and

Copyright © 1991 Grey Dog Music (administered by Williamson Music)
International Copyright Secured   All Rights Reserved

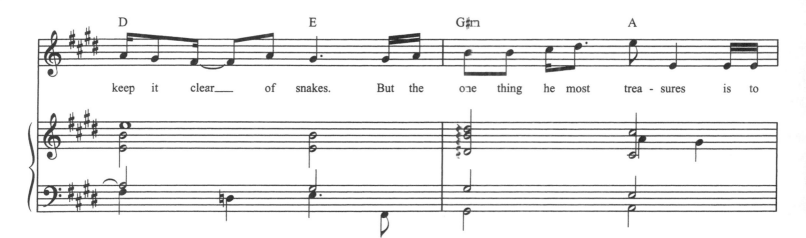

keep it clear___ of snakes. But the one thing he most trea - sures is to

make his own___ mis - takes. Oh . . ._____ He goes

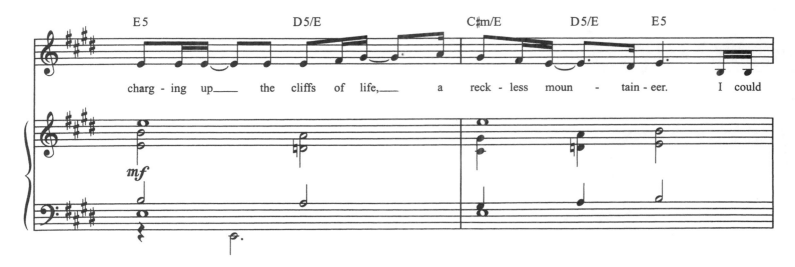

charg - ing up___ the cliffs of life,___ a reck - less moun - tain - eer. I could

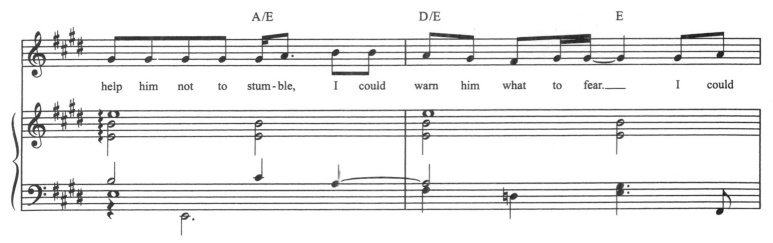

help him not to stum - ble, I could warn him what to fear.___ I could

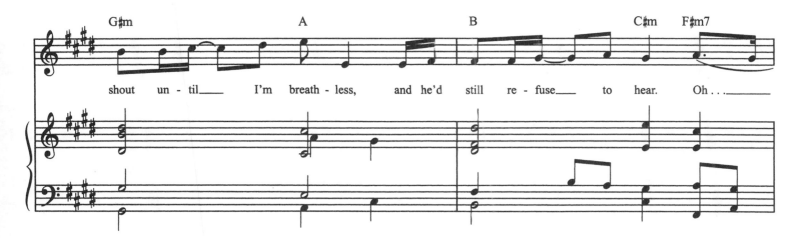

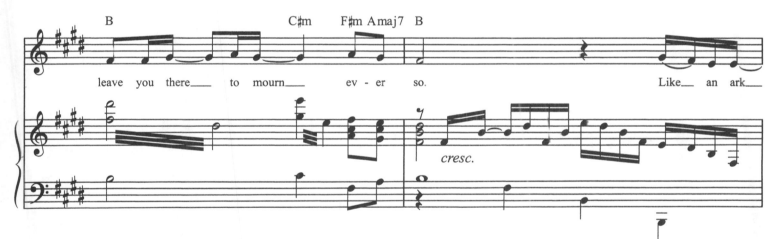

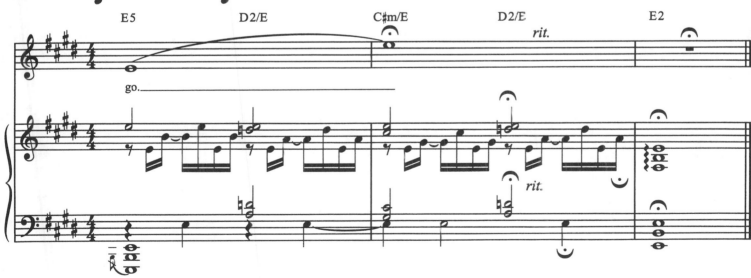

AIN'T IT GOOD?

Music and Lyrics by
STEPHEN SCHWARTZ

Gospel feel (rubato)

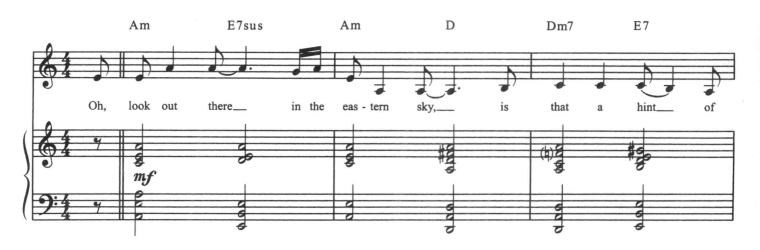

Oh, look out there____ in the eas-tern sky,____ is that a hint____ of

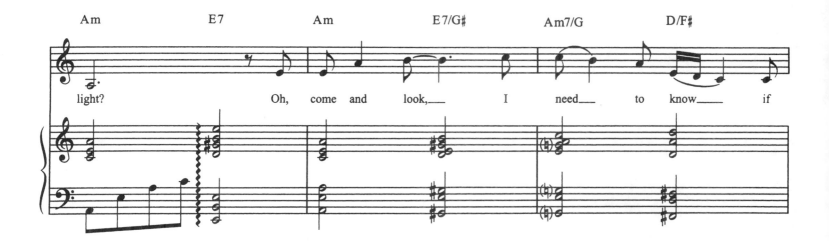

light? Oh, come and look,____ I need____ to know____ if

I am see-ing right. We've lived so long in dark,____ I'm al-most fright-

Copyright © 1991 Grey Dog Music (administered by Williamson Music)
International Copyright Secured All Rights Reserved

75

78

IN THE BEGINNING

Music and Lyrics by
STEPHEN SCHWARTZ

Copyright © 1991 Grey Dog Music (administered by Williamson Music)
International Copyright Secured   All Rights Reserved

prom - ise of the earth in our____ hands . . .

No flood from heav - en comes a - gain.

No del - uge will de - stroy and pur - i - fy.

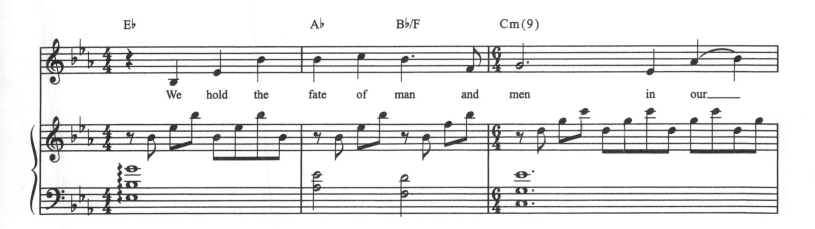

We hold the fate of man and men in our____

82

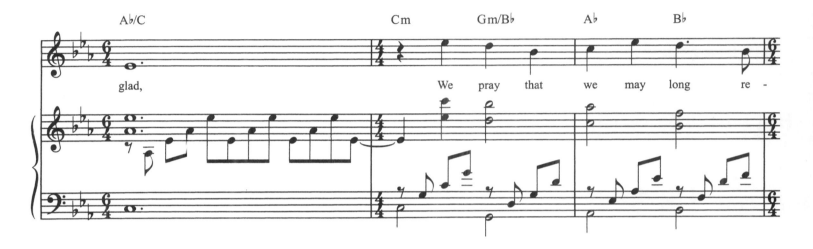

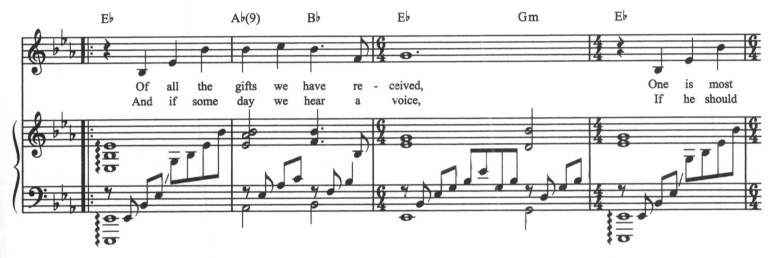

Of all the gifts we have re - ceived, One is most
And if some day we hear a voice, If he should

pre - cious and most ter - ri - ble: The will in
speak a - gain, our si - lent Fa - ther, All He will

each of us is free. It's in our_ hands.
tell us is the

choice   is   in   our   hands.   Our   hands   can

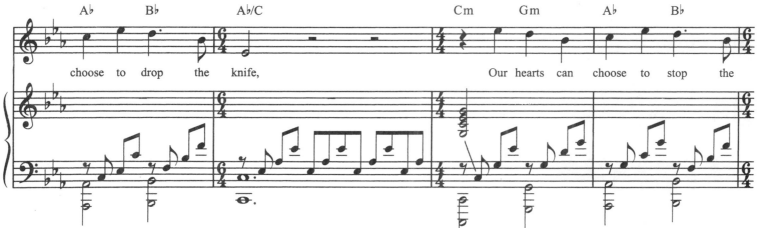

choose   to   drop   the   knife,   Our   hearts   can   choose   to   stop   the

hat - ing.   For   ev - 'ry   mo - ment   of   our

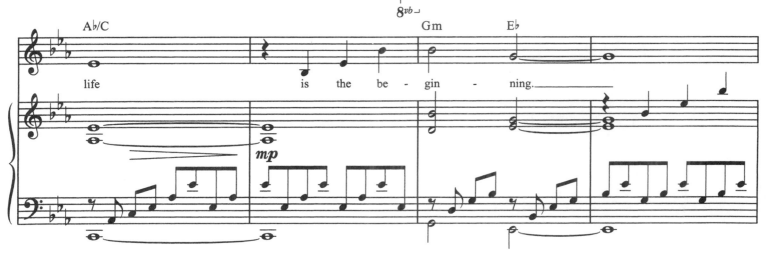

life   is   the   be - gin - ning.

Slightly slower (♩ = 92)

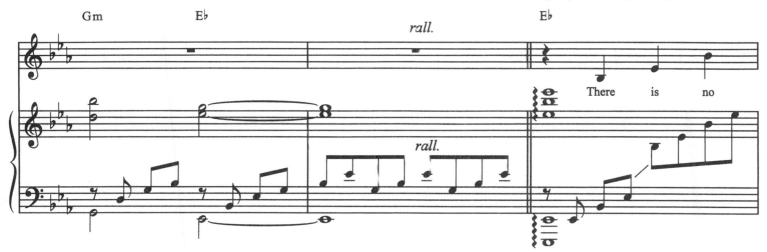

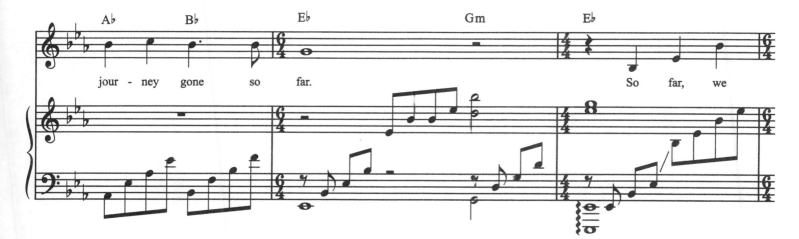

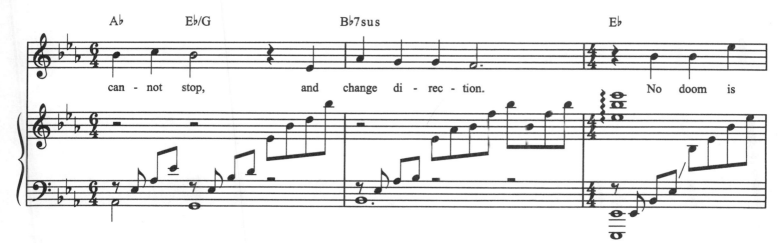

Broader

We can - not know what will oc - cur.

Just make our jour - ney worth the tak - ing.

(Alt. melody) And pray we're wis - er than we were,

poco accel.

in the be - gin - ning.

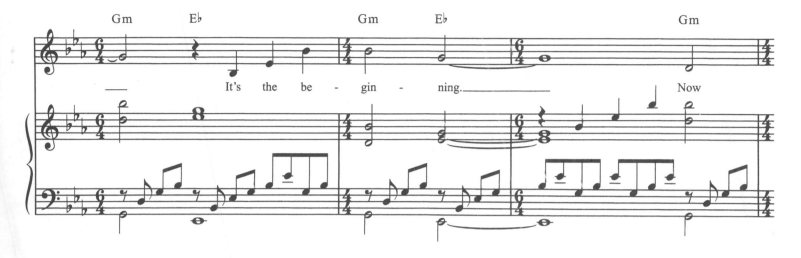

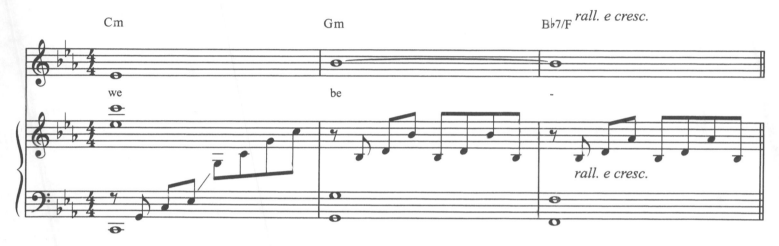

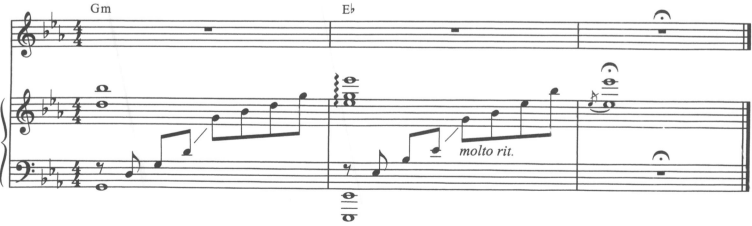